WHITE STAINS

WHITE STAINS

Aleister Crowley

White Stains by Aleister Crowley. Published by Aiwass Books, 2019.

FIRST PRINTING, 2019.

ISBN: 9781697685527.

Contents

THE LITERARY REMAINS OF GEORGE ARCHIBALD BISHOP[1]

A NEUROPATH OF THE SECOND EMPIRE

---

[1] Pseudonym used by Crowley when the manuscript of *White Stains* was first published in Amsterdam, 1898.

Une nouvelle Phèdre a lui moins dure.[2]

---

[2] Translation: "A new, gentler version of Phèdre."

Preface

IN THE FEVERED DAYS AND NIGHTS under the Empire that perished in the struggle of 1870, that whirling tumult[3] of pleasure, scheming, success, and despair,[4] the minds of men had a trying ordeal to pass through. In Zola's *La Curée*[5] we see how such ordinary and natural characters as those of Saccard, Maxime, and the incestuous heroine, were twisted and distorted from their normal sanity, and sent whirling into the jaws of a hell far more *effrayant*[6] than the mere cheap and nasty brimstone Sheol[7] which is a Shibboleth for the dissenter, and with which all classes of religious humbug, from the Pope to the Salvation ranter, from the Mormon and the Jesuit to that mongrel mixture of the worst features of both, the Plymouth Brother, have scared their illiterate, since hypocrisy was born, with Abel, and spiritual tyranny, with Jehovah!

Society, in the long run, is eminently sane and practical; under the Second Empire it ran mad. If these things are done in the green tree of Society, what shall be done in the dry tree of Bohemianism? Art always has a suspicion to fight against; always some poor mad Max Nordau[8] is handy to call everything outside the kitchen the asylum. Here, however, there is a substratum of truth. Consider the intolerable long roll of names, all tainted with glorious madness.

---

[3] The British Empire.

[4] The Franco-Prussian War of 1870–1871; Anglo-Zulu War of 1879-1879; Third Carlist War in Spain 1872–1876, etc.

[5] *La Curée* ['The Kill'] is a novel by Émile Zola published in 1871.

[6] French: "Terrifying."

[7] Hebrew underworld.

[8] Zionist leader Max Simon Nordau (1849–1923).

Baudelaire[9] the diabolist, debauchee of sadism, whose dreams are nightmares, and whose waking hours delirium;[10] Rollinat[11] the necrophile, the poet of phthisis, the anxiomaniac; Péladan, the high priest... of nonsense; Mendes[12], frivolous and scoffing sensualist; besides a host of others, most alike in this, that, below the cloak of madness and depravity, the true heart of genius burns.

No more terrible period than this is to be found in literature; so many great minds, of which hardly one comes to fruition; such seeds of genius, such a harvest of... whirlwind! Even a barren waste of sea is less saddening than one strewn with wreckage.

In England such wild song found few followers of any worth or melody. Swinburne stands on his solitary pedestal above the vulgar crowds of priapistic plagiarists;[13] he alone caught the fierce frenzy of Baudelaire's brandied shrieks, and his First Series of Poems and Ballads was the legitimate echo of that not fierier note. But English Art as a whole was unmoved, at any rate not stirred to any depth, by this wave of debauchery. The great thinkers maintained the even keel, and the windy waters lay nor for their frailer barks to cross.

THERE IS ONE EXCEPTION OF NOTE, till this day unsuspected, in the person of George Archibald Bishop.[14] In a corner of Paris this young poet (for in his nature the flower

---

9 Like Crowley, French poet Charles Pierre Baudelaire (1821–1867) openly took illicit substances and wrote about his experiences. Baudelaire's *Les Fleurs du mal* is widely considered a landmark of modern literature.

10 The delirium is a reference to the French writer's excessive wine drinking and regular opium use.

11 French poet Maurice Rollinat (1846-1903).

12 Brazilian philosopher Raimundo Teixeira Mendes (1855-1927).

13 Swinburne's works explored risqué themes.

14 Meaning Crowley.

of poesy did spring, did even take root and give some promise of a brighter bloom, till stricken and blasted in later years by the lightning of his own sins) was steadily writing day after day, night after night, often working forty hours at a time, work which he destined to entrance the world.

All England should ring with his praises; bye-and-bye the whole world should know his name. Of these works none of the longer and more ambitious remains. How they were lost, and how those fragments we possess were saved, is best told by relating the romantic and almost incredible story of his life.

The known facts of this life are few, vague, and unsatisfactory; the more definite statements lack corroboration, and almost the only source at the disposal of the biographer is the letters of Mathilde Doriac to Madame J. S., who has kindly placed her portfolio at my service. A letter dated Oct. 15th, 1866 indicates that our author was born on the 23rd of that month. The father and mother of George were, at least on the surface, of an extraordinary religious turn of mind. Mathilde's version of the story, which has its source in our friend himself, agrees almost word for word with a letter of the Rev. Edw. Turle to Mrs. Cope, recommending the child to her care. The substance of the story is as follows.

The parents of George carried their religious ideas to the point of never consummating their marriage! This arrangement does not seem to have been greatly appreciated by the wife at least; one fine morning she was found to be enceinte. The foolish father never thought of the hypothesis which commends itself most readily to a man of the world, not to say a man of science, and adopted that of a second Messiah! He took the utmost pains to conceal the birth of the child, treated everybody who came to the house as an emissary of Herod, and finally made up his mind to flee into Egypt! Like most religious maniacs, he never had an idea of his own, but distorted the beautiful and edifying events of the Bible into insane and ridiculous ones, which he proceeded to plagiarize.

On the voyage out the virgin mother became enamoured, as was her wont, of the nearest male, in this case a fellow-traveller. He, being well able to support her in the luxury which she desired, easily persuaded her to leave the boat with him by stealth. A small sailing vessel conveyed them to Malta, where they disappeared. The only trace left in the books of earth records that this fascinating character was accused, four years later, in Vienna, of poisoning her paramour, but thanks to the wealth and influence of her new lover, she escaped.

The legal father, left by himself with a squalling child to amuse, to appease in his tantrums, and to bring up in the nurture and admonition of the Lord, was not a little perplexed by the sudden disappearance of his wife. At first he supposed that she had been translated, but, finding that she had not left the traditional mantle behind her, he abandoned this supposition in favour of a quite different, and indeed a more plausible one.

He now believed her to be the scarlet woman in the Apocalypse, with variations. On arrival in Egypt he hired an old native nurse, and sailed for Odessa. Once in Russia he could find Gog and Magog, and present to them the child as Antichrist. For he was now persuaded that he himself was the First Beast, and would ask the sceptic to count his seven heads and ten horns. The heads, however, rarely totted up accurately!

At this point the accounts of Mr. Turle and Mathilde diverge slightly. The cleric affirms that he was induced by a Tartar lady, of an honourable and ancient profession, to accompany her to Tibet 'to be initiated into the mysteries.' He was, of course, robbed and murdered with due punctuality, in the town of Kiev. Mathilde's story is that he travelled to

Kiev on the original quest, and died of typhoid or cholera. In any case, he died at Kiev in 1839. This fixes the date of the child's birth at 1837.

His faithful nurse conveyed him safely to England, where his relatives provided for his maintenance and education.

With the close of this romantic chapter in his early history we lose all reliable traces for some years. One flash alone illumines the darkness of his boyhood; in 1853, after being prepared for confirmation, he cried out in full assembly, instead of kneeling to receive the blessing of the officiating bishop, 'I renounce forever this idolatrous church'; and was quietly removed.

He told Mathilde Doriac that he had been to Eton and Cambridge; neither institution, however, preserves any record of such admission. The imagination of George, indeed, is tremendously fertile with regard to events in his own life. His own story is that he entered Trinity College, Cambridge, in 1856, and was sent down two years later for an article which he had contributed to some University or College Magazine. No confirmation of any sort is to be found anywhere with regard to these or any other statements of our author.

There is, however, no doubt that in 1861 he quarrelled with his family; went over to Paris, where he settled down, at first, like every tufthead, somewhere in the Quartier Latin; later, with Mathilde Doriac, the noble woman who became his mistress and held to him through all the terrible tragedy of his moral, mental, and physical life, in the Rue du Faubourg-Poissonniere.

At his house there the frightful scenes of '68 took place, and it was there too that he was apprehended after the murders which he describes so faithfully in 'Abysmos.'

He had just finished this poem with a shriek of triumph, and had read it through to the appalled Mathilde 'avec des yeux de flamme et de gestes incoherentes' when, foaming at the mouth, and 'hurlant de blasphemes indicibles', he fell upon her with extraordinary violence of passion; the door opened, officers appeared, the arrest was effected. He was committed to an asylum, for there could be no longer any doubt of his complete insanity; for three weeks he had been raving with absinthe, and satyriasis.

He survived his confinement no long time; the burning of the asylum with its inmates was one of the most terrible events of the war of 1870. So died one of the most talented Englishmen of his century, a man who for wide knowledge of men and things was truly to be envied, yet one who sold his birthright for a mess of beastlier pottage than ever Esau guzzled, who sold soul and body to Satan for sheer love of sin, whose mere lust of perversion is so intense that it seems to absorb every other emotion and interest. Never since God woke light from chaos has such a tragedy been unrolled before men, step after step toward the Lake of Fire!

At his house all his writings were seized, and, it is believed, destroyed. The single most fortunate exception is that of a superbly jewelled writing-case, now in the possession of the present editor, in which were found the MSS. which are here published. Mathilde, who knew how he treasured its contents, preserved it by saying to the officer, 'But, sir, that is mine.'

On opening this it was found to contain, beside these MSS., his literary will. All MSS. were to be published thirty years after his death, not before. He would gain no spurious popularity as a reflection of the age he lived in.

'Tennyson,' he says, 'will die before sixty years are gone by: if I am to be beloved of men, it shall be because my work is for all times and all men, because it is greater than all the gods of chance and change, because it has the heart of the human race beating in every line.

This is a patch of magenta to mauve, undoubtedly; but—
! The present collection of verses will hardly be popular; if
the lost works turn up, of course it may be that there may
be found 'shelter for songs that recede.'

Still, even here, one is, on the whole, more attracted
than repelled; the author has enormous power, and he
never scruples to use it, to drive us half mad with horror, or,
as in his earlier most exquisite works, to move us to the no-
blest thoughts and deeds. True, his debt to contemporary
writers is a little obvious here and there; but these are small
blemishes on a series of poems whose originality is always
striking, and often dreadful, in its broader features.

We cannot leave George Bishop without a word of en-
quiry as to what became of the heroic figure of Mathilde
Doriac. It is a bitter task to have to write in cold blood the
dreadful truth about her death. She had the misfortune to
contract, in the last few days of her life with him, the same
terrible disease which he describes in the last poem of this
collection.

This shock, coming so soon after, and, as it were, as an
unholy perpetual reminder of the madness and sequestra-
tion of her lover, no less than of his infidelity, unhinged her
mind, and she shot herself on July 5th, 1869. Her last letter
to Madame J ... S ... is one of the tenderest and most pa-
thetic ever written.

She seems to have been really loved by George, in his
wild, infidel fashion: 'All Night' and 'Victory', among others,
are obviously inspired by her beauty; and her devotion to
him, the abasement of soul, the prostitution of body, she
underwent for and with him, is one of the noblest stories life
has known. She seems to have dived with him, yet ever try-
ing to raise his soul from the quagmire; if God is just at all,
she shall stand more near to His right hand than the
vaunted virgins who would soil no hem of vesture to save
their brother from the worm that dieth not!

The Works of George Archibald Bishop will speak for themselves; it would be both impertinent and superfluous in me to point out in detail their many and varied excellences, or their obvious faults. The raison d'être, though, of their publication, is worthy of especial notice. I refer to their psychological sequence, which agrees with their chronological order.

His life-history, as well as his literary remains, gives us an idea of the progression of diabolism as it really is; not as it is painted. Note also, (1) the increase of selfishness in pleasure, (2) the diminution of his sensibility to physical charms.

Pure and sane is his early work; then he is carried into the outer current of the great vortex of Sin, and whirls lazily through the sleepy waters of mere sensualism; the pace quickens, he grows fierce in the mysteries of Sapphism and the cult of Venus Aversa with women; later of the same forms of vice with men, all mingled with wild talk of religious dogma and a general exaltation of Priapism at the expense, in particular, of Christianity, in which religion, however, he is undoubtedly a believer till the last (the pious will quote James 2: 19,[15] and the infidel will observe that he died in an asylum); then the full swing of the tide catches him, the mysteries of death become more and more an obsession, and he is flung headlong into Sadism, Necrophilia, all the maddest, fiercest vices that the mind of fiends ever brought up from the pit.

But always to the very end his power is unexhausted, immense, terrible. His delirium does not amuse; it appalls! A man who could conceive as he did must himself have had some glorious chord in his heart vibrating to the eternal

---

[15] *"You believe that there is one God. Good! Even the demons believe that and shudder."* – King James Bible.

principle of Boundless Love. That this love was wrecked is for me, in some sort a relative of his, a real and bitter sorrow. He might have been so great! He missed Heaven! Think kindly of him!

Dédicace

You crown me king and queen. There is a name
For whose soft sound I would abandon all
This pomp. I liefer would have had you call
Some soft sweet title of beloved shame.
Gold coronets be seemly, but bright flame
I choose for diadem; I would let fall
All crowns, all kingdoms, for one rhythmical
Caress of thine, one kiss my soul to tame.

You crown me king and queen; I crown thee lover!
I bid thee hasten, nay, I plead with thee,
Come in the thick dear darkness to my bed.
Heed not my sighs, but eagerly uncover,
As our mouths mingle, my sweet infamy,
And rob thy lover of his maidenhead.

Lie close; no pity, but a little love.
Kiss me but once and all my pain is paid.
Hurt me or soothe, stretch out one limb above
Like a strong man who would constrain a maid.
Touch me; I shudder and my lips turn back
Over my shoulder if so be that thus
My mouth may find thy mouth, if aught there lack
To thy desire, till love is one with us.

God! I shall faint with pain, I hide my face
For shame. I am disturbed, I cannot rise,
I breathe hard with thy breath; thy quick embrace

Crushes; thy teeth are agony—pain dies
In deadly passion. Ah! You come—you kill me!
Christ! God! Bite! Bite! Ah Bite!
Love's fountains fill me.

Prefatory

Sonnet to the Virgin Mary

Mother of God! Who knowest the dire pangs
Of childbirth, and has suffered, and dost know
How utter sweet the full fruit of thy woe,
And how His heel hath crushed the serpent's fangs,
Be with me in the birth of this my book,
These songs of mine, poor children, like to die;
Yet, if they may not perish utterly,
It is to thee for sustenance I look.

Mother of God! Be with me in success,
Abide with me if peradventure fail
These faint songs, murmurs of a summer gale
That my heart clothes within a mortal dress;
And with thy sympathy, their bliss or bale
Shall be too light to shake my happiness.

A Fragment

Man - Hero.
Maid - Heroine.
Her Mother.
Count B.

He: Draw nigh, sweet maiden, violets blush at birth,
Pale lilies tinge with crimson, as the snow
At dawn's approach, the pansy's darksome dye
Deepens when tender winds blow over it
And give its beauties to the summer's gaze:
So blush at being mine, yet gently come
And place a dainty hand within my hold
Too delicate to crush it into warmth,
Save that blood mantling to thy cheek shall flow
Back to the fingers, though I press them not.

And so I will not hesitate to put
A ring upon thy hand, sweet mystery
Of Love's device, to shadow in our hearts
Th' Eternity of an immortal self
That is, and shall be while the stars endure,
Or while a God of Love is pitiful
Of all men's sorrows, and most happy in
Their joys—

She: Ah! Joys are fleeting!

He: But our love
Is anchored in the portals of the dawn
Where heaven begins.

She: And heaven begins with us
This day. Behold the flowers, whose kindly gaze
Of modest love is on us as we stand,
And clasp fond hands before high Heaven to swear
Truth an eternal bond, no parchment scroll
Of perishable matter ill devised
And scored upon with perishable ink,
But in our pulses' quick delight to live
From day to day renewed, as if a fount
Of God's mysterious stream, that here a man
May wet his ankle, and again immerse
Unto his knees, and yet again assay
To cross its silver depth and find himself
Swimming in crystal coldness on a sea
Broad as God's mercy and as deep as Love.

He: And whose strong tide shall bear our spirit out
Into the ocean of all happiness
Whose bounds are Heaven.

She: See! The scythe of Time
Sweeps on to cut the new-born flowers in twain
That symbolizes the reluctant hour
In which we met, and now the flower is dead
And we must part.

He: Fond hearts, chaste souls, as one
Whose unity is sacred, still shall dwell
Together—Not the cold embrace
Of 'We shall meet again,' but let us say
The ritual of a lover, being this
'God be with you!'

She: O heart too dear to me,

Too much beloved for lover's tongue to tell,
God be with you! Farewell, sweet heart!

He: Farewell.

(Exeunt).
Desunt cetera.

The Rainbow

On land wrought of starlight rain lingers
In delicate spirals and spines,
And sunlight's immaculate fingers
Creep through the desire of the pines;
The promise is flashed into being,
Tremendous and florid and proud,
To be seen by the eyes of the seeing,
A bow in the cloud.

O flamed through the sky as a harlot
In splendour transcendent and bold,
With purple and crimson and scarlet
And azure and olive and gold!
O melting to magic and mystery,
As clouds fly to heaven again,
And holy Hyperion's history
Is flashed into rain!

O Godhead of glory through anguish!
O Christ shone through Magdalen's tears!
Thy sons on the universe languish
In iron bands strong as the spheres;
With virtue Thy likeness we cover,
With priestcraft we mock at Thy power,
And the meanest on earth is a lover,
As vile as a flower.

Come down through the visionless ether,
And watch for the sprout of the grain
Hid dark in the wonder beneath her,
A marvel of passion and pain;

Smite power from on high into mortals,
Draw spirit to spirit and higher,
That winds burst the wonderful portals
And tongues as of fire.

O Life of the stars in their glory,
O Light of the passionate spring,
How sweet and supreme is thy story,
Most Wonderful, Counsellor, King!
O crucified, slain, re-arisen!
Burst open the fetters that bind,
Change from us the garb of our prison
And lighten the mind.

O Spring, tell the bountiful Giver
Thy smiles on the world are in vain;
Come down, O Lord God, and deliver
Our souls from the wheel and the chain,
That Love may lie fragrant and shaded,
And Joy may spread wings unto flight,
And Peace stand above, unupbraided,
As splendid as night.

No longer the sun shall cast shadow,
No longer the flower shall lack rain,
The word shall be fair as a meadow,
And Love knows no tincture of pain;
The Glory of God shall be on us,
And over the kingdom unpriced
The Spirit of Love is upon us,
A crucified Christ!

O rapture! O glory! O gladness!
When Satan is fled from the land,
When Christ cleanses sin, and from madness

Deletes its indelible brand;
For life shall spring where they have smitten,
And Love rise from under the rod,
Till all men behold what is written,
The kingdom of God!

With a copy of 'Poems and Ballads'

Bon Pantagruel, je t'offre ces lyriques,
Vu que tu aimes, comme moi, ces mots
Des roideurs sadiques d'un grand jambot,
Des sacrees lysses de l'amour saphique.

Accepte donc comme te moin complet
D'amitié, ce petit don, qui dit
Toutes les délices de rose et lys,
Ces fleurs odorantes du sadinet!

Oublie donc, en lisant, toute faute
De moi qui écris cette dedicace
Faible, d'une lyre mal attunee;

Souviens-toi seul de l'admiration haute
Qui a fait naitre, d'éternelle grace,
La fleur d'une loyale amitié.

Notes

Translation

Dear Pantagruel, I offer you these lyrics,
Since you like, as do I, words that have
The sadistic stiffness of a big ham,
The sacred kisses of Sapphic love.

Please accept my complete friendship,
A little gift which speaks
Of the delights of rose and lily,
Flowers that smell of the sadist!

So forget when reading, the many faults,
From he who writes this dedication
From a poorly tuned lyre;

Remember only the admiration from on high,
From He who gave us life, the eternal grace,
And the flowering of a loyal friendship.

Ad Lydiam, ut Secum a Marito Fugeret

1

The bird has chosen, and the world of spring
Under Love's banner is enrolled, but thou,
Chained to the iron couch of wedlock fast,
Art mourning while all nature else doth sing
The deep delights of Love. Still on thy brow
Lurks the dark shade, thy smile is overcast
With fear of the world's thought, and lips of love
Pale at that spectre, imminent, immense,
Cold Chastity, the child of Impotence,
And eyes grow dim with grey distrust thereof.
Forget, dear heart, forget; life's glow is sweet:
Come to a lover's arms that grow divine
At the first eloquent embrace of thine,
While pulses in wild unison warmly beat.

2

I know a valley walled with glistening steep
Of fire-hewn rock, and stately cliff of ice,
Filled with green lawns and forests black with pine,
Where the clear stream shall sing us into sleep
With murmuring faintly, and divine device:
Come with me there, and we will surely twine
Bright wreaths of Alpine gentian for thine head,
Those glowing tresses, auburn in the sun,
And in the night, dim fires of matchless red
To hold my love, and lead my kisses on
From night to night upon the purple bed

Of dark embraces; till the summer is gone
We will forget in love the world of tears
Whose tumult reaches not our amorous ears.

3

Come with me thither. Let the chaster snow
Blush at the sunset, when our limbs grow faint
To twine close caressing, let it blush
Redder at sunrise, when our eyelids grow
Weary of kissing, and our arms again
Slowly unclasp, and our fair cheeks do flush
With memory's modesty. The mountains glow
Warmer and whiter, dreamland's power shall wane
While the sun tints the beauty of the bush
And all the forest with his finger-tips
Of budding fire, and we surprised will wake
While Shadow's brush in darker colour dips,
And roam about the valley, and will take
Fresh delicate delight, with smiling lips.

4

Summer may die, but on the azure sea
That girdles warmer lands the sun will gleam;
There will we wander, over dale and how,
Sweet with green sward, faint flower, and tender tree.
There all the winter may we idly dream
Still of our love, and there forgetfulness
Of the past sorrow may steal o'er thy brow
In the new birth of stainless happiness,
Rich harvest of the blossoms desire,
Satisfied always, yet forever fresh

In hearts so passionate, and there may'st thou
Love to thy fulness, nor forever tire
Of linking me to thee with dainty mesh
Of auburn ripples of delicious fire.

5

Doubt not, dear love, nor hesitate to say;
Blush if thou wilt; I love to see thy cheek
Grow hot with love-thoughts—let the word be said:
Between shy finger whisper me the 'yea!'
My soul will leap to hear, as thine to speak.
Remember Love, forget the loveless bed;
Forget thy husband, and the cruel wreck
Of thy dear life on Wedlock's piteous sands;

Love's all in all, link on the golden bands
Forged in heaven without flaw or fleck.
I know thine answer by these amorous hands
That touch me thus to tempt me, by the kiss
Whose sudden passion burns upon my neck
Thy heart clings to me in perfect 'Yes!'

Contra Conjugium T.B.B.

Anathema foederis nefandi, jugeris immondi, flagitii contra Amorem, contra Naturam, contra Deum, in saecula praesit Amen! Cum comminatione pastorum improborum, Ecclesiae malae, qui tales nuptias benedicunt.

Through nave and chancel drone the choir,
Their chant rolls through the darkened aisle;
Their song soars up beyond the spire;
The priest prepares; there waits his smile
A deed most vile.

Harken, thou fool at altar-rails
The still small awful voice of fear
Whereat earth shakes and heaven pales—
'I am the Lord'; His voice rings clear:
'What dost thou here?

'Thou hast despised my laws, and stilled
The voice of Nature and my voice,
Now, shall thy life with joy be filled?
At thine own time shalt thou rejoice?
At thine own choice?

'I gave thee life, I gave thee youth,
Four seasons fair, for love the same,
Health, strength and comeliness—forsooth,
And thou hast quenched my holy flame,
And scorned my name!

'I gave thee life, life passeth by;
I gave thee youth, that youth is fled.
Thinkst thou that I will fructify
Now, at thine own good time, thy dead
And barren bed?

'How worship me, yet break my laws?
Art thou a God? Didst thou devise
The infinite world? Did thy word cause
The silver Caucasus to arise?
Art thou all-wise?

'Or hast thou mocked me, setting high
A molten calf, a graven block,
A fetish foul, a devil's lie,
And worshipped that? Thou shalt not mock,
Thou barren rock!

'Thou shalt not mock! Cold Chastity,
Father and child of Impotence,
Whom thou hast set on high for me,
From her foul shrine shall chase thee thence:
'Avoid, get hence!'

'And I—thou shalt not scorn my word,
All Nature sets its scorn on thee;
Sweet flower and stream, swift fish and bird,
Shall chorus out 'Thou fruitless tree!
Thou salt dry sea!'

'I will not aid thee in thine age,
Nor heed thee in thy piteous strait;
Live thou in thine own empty cage,
Forged every day that thou didst wait
Too long, too late!

'Shall I turn back the seasons past,
Recall sun's shine and cloudlet's fleece,
Revive the ghosts of aeons vast,
And bid the scythe of Chronos cease
For thy caprice?

'Because thou wilt, shall I accede
And change my laws that I have made
Shall I make grapes from thorn and weed,
Fresh water from the fountains stayed,
If thou hast prayed?

'For thine outcry bring chaos back,
Turn over earth and heaven to hell,
And listen 'mid the roar and wrack,
With pleasure to creation's knell,
Thy marriage bell?

'I will not turn the Red Sea back
That thou mayst pass again dry-shod:
Thou hast chosen, thou shalt live the black
Dry years out till thou cleave the sod,
And meet thy God.

'What are thy good deeds? This one thing
Thou hast not done. This chiefest task
Thou wouldst not do. And shall the King
Of Kings do only what men ask?
Thou empty mask!

'Repentance is too late, lost fool,
Dead flower, salt fountain, rusty sword,
This curse is on thee for thy dule,
That thou shalt know and be assured
I am the Lord.'

The loud-voiced choir would drown in song
The voice of God; their music woke
Echoes through chancel weird and long—
In thunder and fierce fire and smoke
Jehovah spoke.

'On with the farce! My perjured priests,
The wolves that raven through my flock,
Nay, wolves in shepherd's garb, wild beasts
That fang and tear my lambs, and mock
At Judah's stock.

'On with the grim foul farce! Black hell
Gapes to receive all actors there.
Play on its brink! What soul can tell
But I, your God, may be as air,
A children's snare?

'But I am here, I will not heed,
I will not give more signs; But I
Will come with heavy hand and deed
And give men knowledge ere they die
How their priests lie.

'A gospel marred, a bastard creed,
A dogma out of hell ye teach!
False shepherds, ye shall learn your meed;
Not as waves breaking on the beach
My wrath shall reach!

'I forget not—heed not my cry,
Play out the farce, wed fast the twain!—
Red judgment and black death draw nigh,
Your blasphemies shall all be vain,

And your souls slain.

'Vipers! On him my mercy falls
Perchance, at last, in heaven; but ye
I will sepulchre in black walls
Of Hell, burn up and hide from me
'Neath the blind sea!

'Vipers! Eternal fire shall quench
Your prayers and curses, hell shall hold
The vapourous vomit of your stench
Wrung from foul souls, no longer bold
But cowed and cold.

'Vipers! His folly I will heal,
Your sin I will not put away;
My Christ is vain for you; appeal
In vain to his shed blood; nor pray
I will not slay.

'I will most utterly destroy
Your souls from off the earth; your power
Sealed by your Satan I will cloy
With subtle strength; your church shall flower
No further hour.

'Because ye set your hands to this,
Blaspheming nature and my name,
Cemented the unholy kiss
Of barren age's fruitless shame
Your hell shall flame

'Seven times more hot, that ye may know
My paths shall be most surely trod,
That I who answer thus, who show

Myself in wielding sword and rod,
Am high Lord God!'

Silent the voice, and through the nave
And chancel droned the choir; the sun
Darkened, as Satan's perjured slave,
The priest, in blessing, made them one.
The Deed was done.

A Ballad of Choosing

Love brought a garland to my feet today
Offering to crown my head withal, and said:
'The year is young, it is the time of May,
Autumn is distant, and the winter, dead '
And would therewith my brows have garlanded
But that I asked him 'Is not this a fire
To burn the scorched brain through my
maddened head?
Thou has a guerdon, is it not for hire?'

Fame brought a golden crown, bejewelled o'er
With precious rubies beyond price, and cried
'The world is young, thy name shall evermore
Ring in men's ears, stately and glorified'
But I, with shuddering lips, to him replied
'Fame is the amaranth that fools desire
My soul's price is beyond thy jewel's pride
Thou has a guerdon, is it not for hire?'

'Wealth brought to me a purse, whose glancing gold
Mocked the sun's rays, grown dull as iron rust,
And pressed it in my hand, saying 'Behold
The corner-stone of fame, the means of lust'
And I 'In thee I put but little trust
Shameful, most vile, accursed of God's ire,
Dross of the dunghill's most detested dust,
Thou has a guerdon, is it not for hire?'

Christ came to me, alone and sorrowful,
And offered me a cross, saying to me,
'I have great joys to give most bountiful.

Carry this through the world, and when the sea
Of death is past, then is prepared for thee
A house of many mansions.' My desire
Hid not from me the vileness of his plea:—
'Thou has a guerdon, is it not for hire?'

Envoi

Prince of the air, thou offerest nought to me
I serve thee, recompensed of hell-fire,
More nobly than these others, verily
Since none with impious word may mock at thee
'Thou has a guerdon, is it not for hire?'

A Jealous Lover

1

I have an idol wrought of stainless gold
Before whose feet I bow, in whose delight
I am content to live, whose spells of might
Are smiles that gleam, are tears that glisten cold
On the fair cheek that blushes if I praise;
Are warm ripe kisses in the softer hours
When love is perfect blossom of sweet flowers,
Are shadowed glances of pure lovelight rays
From clear blue eyes, are wonderful caresses
When love is golden autumn of sweet fruit.
What other worship can usurp my days
When I may lie amid her sunny tresses
Enraptured by the music of her lute
One long calm love, one heart's delight always?

2

Bright spheres of heaven, firefly gleams, fair ghosts
Laugh lightly to the silver globe of night
That glitters on green fields, and on the sea
Ripples break foamless, where the golden coasts
Echo their mellow cadence. Such delight
Is on me I would fain sigh into sleep
Until my love comes forth to dream with me
Of silent words of love and peopled stars
Where we may live and love and never weep
Nor yet be weary. The last ruby bars
Are sunk beneath the sea. The shadows creep

More on me as I quicken with desire
My love is all of gold, my faith is deep
Lit with my heart's imperishable fire.

3

Pale spectres of the stars, corpse-lights, bad-ghosts
Sicken the icy glamour of the moon
Upon the vacant earth; and where the sea
Marshals sepulchral billows, obscene hosts
Of harpies gibber weirdly. I should swoon
For the silence, rolled not some dread minstrelsy
In fearful anguish on the shuddering air,
Breathing out terror and lightning to the night
That wildly echoes back Hell's venomous spite,
And shrieks aloud the watchword of despair
To draw each painracked nerve more tense and gray
For I am alone, unloved, in murk and gloom,
Unloved, unfriended, fittest for the tomb,
Who worshipped golden feet and found them clay.

4

She creeps alive upon the tawny sands,
False glittering woman, girt about with lies!
She steals toward me, the tigress sleek and fierce!
Destroying devil, with long sinuous hands
And hate triumphant in blue-murderous eyes!
I nerve myself to spring upon and pierce
With maddening fangs those firm white bosom
towers,
To tear those lithe voluptuous limbs apart
And glut my ravening soul with vengeance. Heart

Quickens as she draws near; the scent of flowers
Breathes round her damned presence. Shall she live
To triumph with those tainted lips of song—
She whispered 'Dearest, I have kept thee long'.
I flung myself before her, 'Love, forgive!'

Ballade de la Jolie Marion

It is a sweet thing to be loved,
Although my sighs in absence wake,
Although my saddening heart is moved,
I smile and bear for love's dear sake.
My songs their wonted music make,
Joyous and careless, songs of youth,
Because the sacred lips of both
Are met to kiss the last good-bye,
Because sweet glances weep for ruth
That we must part, and love must die.

Remembrance of love's long delights
Is to remember sighs and tears,
Yet I will think upon the nights
I whispered into passionate ears
The fond desires, the sweet faint fears.
My lover's limbs of lissome white
Gleamed in the darkness and strange light,
The wondrous orbs voluptuously
Bent on me all unearthly bright:
But we must part, and love must die.

Fond limbs with mine were intertwined,
A hand lascivious fondled me;
My ears grew deaf, my eyes grew blind,
My tongue was hot from kisses free,
Short madness, and we lazily
Lolled back upon the bed of fire.
I was a-weary—her desire

Drew her upon me—Marion, fie!
You work our pleasure till I tire:
But we must part, and love must die.

Nor thus did love's embraces wane,
Though lusty limbs grow idle quite;
Our mouths' red valves are over-fain
To suck the sweetness from the night;
And amorously, with touches light,
Steal passion from reluctant pain.
So has the daystar fled again
Before the blushes of the sky,
So did I clasp thy knees in vain:
For we must part, and love must die.

You say another's sensuous lips
Shall open to my kisses there:
When weary, steal those luscious sips;
Another's hands play in my hair
And find delight for me to bare
The bosom, and the passionate mound
White and, for Venus' temple, round,
A garden of wild thyme whose eye
My sword shall piece, and never wound:
For we must part, and love must die.

You say—but Oh! My Marion's kiss
Shall linger on my palate still,
No joy on earth is like to this
That we have tasted to our fill
Of all our sweet lascivious will.
The cup is drained of lust's delight,

Yet wells with pleasure, and by night
I'll come once more and loving lie
Between thine amorous limbs, despite
That we must part and love must die.

Envoi

Thus, sweet, I'll sing when day doth break
And weary lovers must awake
To part, but now our pleasure take
In one last bout of rivalry,
Whose passions first shall answer make
To the dances that the curtains shake
Till we must part and love must die.

At Stockholm

We could not speak, although the sudden glow
Of passion mantling to the crimson cheek
Of either, told our tale of love, although
We could not speak.

What need of language, barren and false and bleak,
While our white arms could link each other so,
And fond red lips their partners mutely seek?

What time for language, when our kisses flow
Eloquent, warm, as words are cold and weak?
Or now; Ah! Sweetheart, even were it so
We could not speak!

Mathilde

O large lips opening outward like a flower
To breathe upon my face that clings to thee!
O wanton breasts that heave deliciously
And tempt my eager teeth! Oh cruel power
Of wide deep thighs that make me furious
As they enclasp me and swing to and fro
With passion that grows pale and drives the flow
Of the fast fragrant blood of both of us
Into the awful link that knits us close
With chain electric! O have mercy yet
In drawing out my life in this desire
To consummate this moment all the gross
Lusts of tonight, and pay the sudden debt
That with strong water shall put out our fire![16]

---

[16] Mathilde was the name of abbess of England's Essen Abbey, 971-1011.

Yet Time to Turn

Brighter than snow on glittering Alps, the soul
Of my lost love was, bluer than the haze
Of those same hills, more violent and deep
Her eyes' clear gaze,
Dreaming of hidden wonders; and the goal
Of life grew luminous o'er Time's empurpled steep.

She loved me then; she loves me now, afar.
Ah, she knew not! And I, so steeped and stained
With fierce sins, knew myself unworthy of
The heart I gained,
And, a lost mariner whose polar star
He is ashamed to look to, cast away her love.

I would not have her love a thing so vile,
I would not link her life with such as mine!
O cursed sin, to leave my soul too high
To cheat the shrine!
I drove Love forth, Love lingered yet awhile
So that I might not quite win Hell before I die.

O little root of nobleness left thus
Dead since it has no power to grow, to bloom;
Live, since I may not bury it within
The gaping tomb
Where virtue lies, that I, imperious,
Long since interred with hope, and all life's joy
save sin.

All Night

All night no change, no whisper. Scarce a breath
But lips closed hard upon the cup of death
To drain its sweetest poison. Scarce a sigh
Beats the dead hours out; scarce a melody
Of measured pulses quickened with the blood
Of that desire which pours its deadly flood
Through soul and shaken body; scarce a thought
But sense through spirit most divinely wrought
To perfect feeling; only through the lips
Electric ardour kindles, flashes, slips
Through all the circle to her lips again
And thence, unwavering, flies to mine, to drain
All pleasure in one draught. No whispered sigh,
No change of breast, love's posture perfectly
Once gained, we change no more. The fever grows
Hotter or cooler, as the night wind blows
Fresh gusts of passion on the outer gate.
But we, in waves of frenzy, concentrate
Our thirsty mouths on that hot drinking cup
Whence we may never suck the nectar up
Too often or too hard; fresh fire invades
Our furious veins, and the unquiet shades
Of night make noises in the darkened room.

Yet, did I raise my head, throughout the gloom
I might behold thine eyes as red as fire,
A tigress maddened with supreme desire.
White arms that clasp me, fervent breast that glides
An eager snake, about my breast and sides,
And white teeth keen to bite, red tongue that tires,
And lips ensanguine with unfed desires,

Hot breath and hands, dishevelled hair and head,
Thy fevered mouth like snakes' mouths crimson red,
A very beast of prey; and I like thee,
Fiery, unweary, as thou art of me.
But raise no head; I know thee, breast and thigh,
Lips, hair and eyes and mouth: I will not die
But thou come with me o'er the gate of death.
So, blood and body furious with breath
That pants through foaming kisses, let us stay
Gripped hard together to keep life away,
Mouths drowned in murder, never satiate,
Kissing away the hard decrees of Fate,
Kissing insatiable in mad desire
Kisses whose agony may never tire,
Kissing the gates of hell, the sword of God,
Each unto each a serpent or a rod,
A well of wine and fire, each unto each,
Whose lips are fain convulsively to reach
A higher heaven, a deeper hell. Ah! Day
So soon to dawn, delight to snatch away!
Damned day, whose sunlight finds us as with wine
Drunken, with lust made manifest divine
Devils of darkness, servants unto hell—
Yea, king and queen of Sheol, terrible
Above all fiends and furies, hating more
The high Jehovah, loving Baal Peor,
Our father and our lover and our god!
Yea, though he lift his adamantine rod
And pierce us through, how shall his anger tame
Fire that glows fiercer for the brand of shame
Thrust in it; so, we who are all of fire,
One dull red flare of devilish desire,
The God of Israel shall not quench with tears,
Nor blood of martyrs drawn from myriad spheres,
Nor watery blood of Christ; that blood shall boil

With all the fury of our hellish toil;
His veins shall dry with heat; his bones shall bleach
Cold and detested, picked of dogs, on each
Dry separate dunghill of burnt Golgotha.
But we will wrest from heaven a little star,
The Star of Bethlehem, a lying light
Fit for our candle, and by devils' might
Fix in the vast concave of hell for us
To lume its ghastly shadows murderous,
That in the mirror of the lake of fire

We may behold the image of Desire
Stretching broad wings upon us, and may leap
Each upon other, till our bodies weep
Thick sweet salt tears, and, clasping as of yore
Within dull limits of Earth's barren shore,
Fulfil immense desires of strange new shames,
Burn into one another as the flames
Of our hell fuse us into one wild soul:
Then, one immaculate divinest whole,
Plunge, fire, within all fire, dive far to death;
Till, like king Satan's sympathetic breath,
Burn on us as a voice from far above
Strange nameless elements of fire and love;
And we, one mouth to kiss, one soul to lure,
Forever, wedded, one, divine, endure
Far from sun, sea, and spring from love or light,
Imbedded in impenetrable night;
Deeper than ocean, higher than the sky,
Vaster than petty loves that dream and die,
Insatiate, angry, terrible for lust,
Who shrivel God to adamantine dust
By our fierce gaze upon him, who would strive
Under our wrath, to flee away, to dive
Into the deep recesses of his heaven.

But we, one joy, one love, one shame for leaven,
Quit hope and life, quit fear and death and love,

Implacable as God, desired above
All loves of hell or heaven, supremely wed,
Knit in one soul in one delicious bed
More hot than hell, more wicked than all things,
Vast in our sin, whose unredeeming wings
Rise o'er the world, and flap for lust of death,
Eager as anyone that travaileth;
So in our lusts, the monstrous burden borne
Heavy within the womb, we wait the morn
Of its fulfilment. Thus eternity
Wheels vain wings round us, who may never die,
But cling as hard as serpent's wedlock is,
One writhing glory, an immortal kiss.

Ode to Venus Callipgye

Where was light when thy body came
Out of the womb of a perished prayer?
Where was life when the sultry air,
Hot with the lust of night and shame,
Brooded on dust, when thy shoulders bare
Shone on the sea with a sudden flame
Into all Time to abundant fame?

CHORUS

Daughter of Lust by the foam of the sea!
Mother of flame! Sister of shame!
Tiger that Sin nor her son cannot tame!
Worship to thee! Glory to thee!
Venus Callipyge, mother of me.

Fruitless foam of a sterile sea,
Wanton waves of a vain desire,
Maddening billows flecked with fire,
Storms that lash on the brine, and flee,
Dead delights, insatiate ire
Broke like a flower to the birth of thee,
Venus Callipgye, mother of me!

Deep wet eyes that are violet-blue!
Haggard cheeks that may blush no more!
Body bruised daintily, touched of gore
Where the sharp fierce teeth have bitten through
The olive skin that thy sons adore,
That they die for daily, are slain anew

By manifold hate; for their tale is few.

Few are thy sons, but as fierce as dawn,
Rapturous moments and weary days,
Nights when thine image a thousand ways
Is smitten and kissed on the fiery lawn
Where the wash of the waves of thy native bays
Laps weary limbs, that of thee have drawn
Laughter and fire for their souls in pawn.

O thy strong sons! They are dark as night,
Cruel and barren and false as the sea,
They have cherished Hell for the love of thee,
Filled with thy lust and abundant might,
Filled with the phantom desire to free
Body and soul from the sound and sight
Of a world and a God that doth not right.

O thy dark daughter! Their breasts are slack,
Their lips so large and as poppies red;
They lie in a furious barren bed;
They lie on their faces, their eyelids lack
Tears, and their cheeks are as roses dead;
White are their throats, but upon the back
Red blood is clotted in gouts of black.

All on their sides are the wounds of lust,
Down, from the home of their auburn hair
Down to the feet that we find so fair;
Where the red sword has a secret thrust
Pain, and delight, and desire they share.
Verily, pain! And thy daughters trust
Thou canst bid roses spring out of dust.

Mingle, ye children of such a queen,

Mingle, and meet, and sow never a seed!
Mingle, and tingle, and kiss and bleed
With the blood of the life of the Lampsacene,
With the teeth that know never a pitiful deed
But fret and foam over with kisses obscene—
Mingle and weep for what years have been.

Never a son nor a daughter grow
From your waste limbs, lest the goddess weep;
Fill up the ranks from the babes that sleep
Far in the arms of a god of snow.
Conquer the world that her throne may keep
More of its pride, and its secret woe
Flow through all earth as the rivers flow.

Which of the gods is like thee, our queen?
Venus Callipyge, nameless, nude,
Thou with the knowledge of all imbued
Secrets of life and the dreams that mean
Loves that are not, as are mortals', hued
All rose and lily, but linger unseen
Passion-flowers purpled, garlands of green!

Who like thyself shall command our ways?
Who has such pleasures and pains for hire?
Who can awake such a mortal fire
In the veins of a man, that deathly days
Have robbed of the masteries of desire?
Who can give garlands of fadeless bays
Unto the sorrow and pain we praise?

Yea, we must praise, though the deadly shade
Fall on the morrow, though fires of hell
Harrow our vitals; a miracle
Springs at thy kisses, for thou hast made

Anguish and sorrow desirable
Torment of hell as the leaves that fade
Quickly forgotten, despised, decayed.

They are decayed, but thou springest again,
Mother of mystery, barren, who bearest
Flowers of most comeliest children, who wearest
Wounds for delight, whose desire shall stain
Star-space with blood as the price thou sharest
With thy red lovers, whose passing pain
Ripens to marvellous after-gain.

Thou art the fair, the wise, the divine,
Thou art our mother, our goddess, our life,
Thou art our passion, our sorrow, our strife,
Thou, on whose forehead no lights ever shine,
Thou, our Redeemer, our mistress, our wife,
Thou, barren sister of deathlier brine,
Venus Callipyge, mother of mine!

CHORUS

Daughter of Lust by the foam of the sea!
Mother of flame! Sister of shame!
Tiger the Sin nor her son cannot tame!
Worship to thee! Glory to thee!
Venus Callipyge, mother of me.

Volupte

Clitoridette, m'amourette,
Ote ta jolie robe d'or,
Tes roses bas, chemise nette,
Et decouvre pour moi le con,
Le con que j'aime, aux cheveux noirs,
Le cul ou tu m'admets ce soir,
Les seins je baise, que j'adore,
Tous les secrets de ton boudoir.

'Viens à moi, qui, raide, couche,
Attendant tes désirs lubriques;
Tu suces et couvres dans la bouche
De l'amour le pouce phallique;
Je tremble, en mourant avec feu,
Voyant la clarté de tes yeux,
Leur flamme méchante, saphique,
Brulant en langueur amoureux.

Laisse mon épée affaiblie,
Donne à mes baisere la vagine
D'où je suc'rai de l'eau-de-lys,
Et te ferai comme divine.
La langue qui cherche tes reins,

Les genoux qui pressent tes seins,
Te feraient déesse, ma mine,
Je mordrai, et tu cries en vain.

Alors, de nouvelle énergie,
Je jette entre tes jolies cuisses,
Dedans ton cul, ce fleur-de-lys,

Long, gros, et ardent. Ça, il glisse
En haut, en bas. La passion croit
Fiévreux, furieux, pour toi!
Vient, la crise du délice! ....
Ah, je suis mort! .... Embrasse-moi!

Rondels

1

Maid of dark eyes, that glow with shy sweet fire,
Song lingers on thy beauty till it dies
In awe and longing on the smitten lyre:
Maid of dark eyes.

Grant me thy love, earth's last surpassing prize,
Me, cast upon the faggots of love's pyre
For love of the white bosom that underlies

The subtle passion of thy snowy attire,
The shadowy secret of thine amorous thighs,
The inmost shrine of my supreme desire,
Maid of dark eyes!

2

Boy of red lips, pale face, and golden hair,
Of dreamy eyes of love, and finger-tips
Rosy with youth, too fervid and too fair,
Boy of red lips.

How the fond ruby rapier glides and slips
'Twixt the white hills thou spreadest for me there;
How my red mouth immortal honey sips

From thy ripe kisses, and sucks nectar rare
When each the shrine of God Priapus clips
In hot mouth passionate more than man may bear,

Boy of red lips![17]

---

[17] The Old French rondel, a version of a *rondeau*, was verse of typically thirteen or four-teen lines set in three stanzas.

60

Ad Lucium

The Lampsacene is girt with golden dress;
His courts gleam ever with forbidden light;
I only bring no gift to him tonight,
Being the mockery of his rod's distress.
While satyrs woo, and fauns, and nymphs give ear,
I burn unslaked, my Lucius is unkind,
He dare not guess, I dare not speak my mind,
Nor feed upon his lips, nor call him dear,
Nor may I clasp him, lissome and divine,
Nor suck our passion from his eager verge,
Nor pleasure in his quick embraces prove;
I faint for love, come aid me sparkling wine,
That my unquenchable desire may urge
In Lucius' fiery heart responsive love.

O fervent and sweet to my bosom
Past woman, I'll clasp thee and cling
Till the buds of desire break to blossom
And my kisses surprise thee and sting;
Till my hand and my mouth are united
In caresses that shake thee and smite,
While the stars hide their lustre affrighted
In measureless night.

I will neither delay nor dissemble
But utter my love in thine ear
Though my voice and my countenance tremble
With a passion past pity and fear;
I will speak from my heart till thou listen
With the soft sound of wings of a dove,
Till thine eyes answer back till they glisten

O Lucius, love!

I will touch thee but once with a finger,
But thy vitals shall shudder and smart,
And the smile through thy sorrow shall linger,
And the touch shall pierce through to thine heart;
Thy lips a denial shall fashion,
Thou shalt tremble and fear to confess,
Till thou suddenly break into passion
With yes, love, and yes.

I will kiss thee and fondle and woo thee
And mingle my lips into thine
That shall tingle and thrill through and through thee
As the draught of the flame of a wine;
I will drink of the fount of our pleasure
Licking round and about and above
Till its streams pour me out their full measure,
O Lucius, love!

Thou shalt clasp me and clamber above me
And press me with eager desire,
Thou shalt kiss me and clip me and love me
With a love beyond infinite fire,
Thou shalt pierce to the portals of passion
And satiate thy longing and lust
In the fearless Athenian fashion,
A rose amid dust.

We will taste all delights and caresses
And know all the secrets of joy,
From the love-look that chastity blesses
To the lusts that deceive and destroy;
We will live in the light of sweet glances,
By day and by night we will move

To the music of manifold dances,
O Lucius, love!

A Paean in the Springtide

Now is the triumph of Love, now is the day of his guerdon,
Now when the blossoms are full on the bountiful delicate spray;
Now has the year sprung aloft and shaken the frost and its burden,
April is come with his showers, sun laughs and promises May.
Newly the bird sings of Love, newly he wooeth a maiden,
Newly the heart of a boy leaps, and his eyes catch its fire.
Light is his laugh as the sea, with no sad remembrances laden;
Light as the sea, and as fierce and fickle is grown his desire.
Here in the spring we are free, as the winds that look love at the ocean;
Change we and weary too soon of delight that is hardly begun;
Pleasure and pain are made one, a delirious noble emotion;
Love dies before he grows manly, dawn never yields to the sun.

Love in a night shall live and die,
Love in a day shall wing and fly;
Love in the Spring shall last an hour,
Easily fades a spring-tide flower.

Where are the blooms of frost, hoary and bright and ves-
tal;
Virginal lips not kissed, flowers unbidden to bud?
Ah! we have slain their beams, as our low heads lazily
nestle,
Where the dark home of Love is, where the impatient
blood

Spurts at the furious kiss, darts far forth as an adder,
Stinging and biting amain, as the night becomes golden
with fire.
Dawn brings reason back, and the violet eyes grow sad-
der,
Eyes that were red in the dark, eyes of enfevered desire.
Eyes that wrote songs with a glance, whose look sang
the sweetest of stories,
Sweeter than lips could have told, who loved better only
to kiss;
Sweeter than hands could have written, who took delight
in the glories
Fierce of a triple embrace, a fadeless implacable bliss.

Love is a sword whose blade is red,
Love is a deed whose fruit is dead;
Love is a tiger, fierce of power,
Easily fades a spring-tide flower.

Death shall come slow and soft, with the stealthy tread
of a leopard;
While the few stars have grown dim, as he seeks for an
innocent prey.
Death shall pounce soon on the fold, where Love was a
treacherous shepherd;
So with hot lips shall he come, ere the mountains are
silver and grey.

Life shall gasp out in the gloom, and all our desires shall perish; Hope and its roseate crown shall fall in the dark to the dust.
Love and his garland shall go, with the last of the joys we may cherish,

Death with cold finger shall touch the delicate springs of our lust.
We shall be weary of kisses, weary of all the caresses
Man or his sisters of shame dream or devise or obtain;
Cover the white limbs ashamed with the fiery impassionate tresses,
Once for a bed to delight, now for a covering to pain.

Love is a fruit with rotted core,
Love is a thing shall be no more;
Love is a bride of a bitter dower,
Easily fades a spring-tide flower.

Where shall be Hylas then? for His lonely lips are sighing,
Vainly in hell for love, vainly for days gone by;
Where the incarnate flame of Lesbian lovers dying,
Then where the world is past, and Heaven or hell draw nigh?
Heaven with cold and loveless lips, though his fruits be many,
Hell with his red mouth hot, barren although he be.
Hylas and Sappho choose, and are never denied of any,
Hell's most insatiate fangs, death and his empery.
Heaven is bare and bleak, hell has the joys beyond Heaven,
Fire and desire and delight, of a love that is always young;

Hell has the pains of hell, but the sweetest of lusts for leaven.

Fierce body, breasts of delight, fearful and murderous tongue.

Hell is the house of all delight,
Heaven the home of a bitter blight;
Pain is our joy and our spirits' power,
Never shall fade its fiery flower.

Now is the triumph of Love, gazing far to an infinite pleasure,

Pleasure that mocks Heaven's hopes, that our hands are impatient to hold.

Love and delight pouring out, in a fearless insatiate measure,

Out of the chalice of lust, scarlet o'errunning its gold.

This is the song of the Spring, that the nightingales carol by starlight,

This the delight of our eyes, as they shine with strange fire in the night,

This is our trust and our joy—beyond death we look on to the far light

Flaming from hell our last home, this is the key of our might.

Come, fiery birds of a clime we know not, and sing us your paean;

Triumph of gods that are known secretly, not by a name,

Gods whose implacable feet have trampled the god Galilean,

Cast though they be into hell, given to death and to shame.

Heaven and hell has striven in war,

Sappho and Hylas, with Christ and Jah;
We are of those, though they lose their power,
Never shall fade their fiery flower.

To J. L. D.

At last, so long desired, so long delayed,
The step is taken, and the threshold past;
I am within the palace I have prayed
At last.

Like scudding winds, when skies are overcast,
Came the soft breath of Love, that might not fade.
O Love, whose magic whispers bind me fast,

O Love, who hast the kiss of Love betrayed,
Hide my poor blush beneath thy pinions vast,
Since thou hast come, nor left me more a maid,
At last.

A Ballad of Passive Pederasty

Of man's delight and man's desire
In one thing is no weariness—
To feel the fury of the fire,
And writhe within the close caress
Of fierce embrace, and wanton kiss,
And final nuptial done aright,
How sweet a passion, shame, is this,
A strong man's love is my delight!

Free women cast a lustful eye
On my gigantic charms, and seek
By word and touch with me to lie,
And vainly proffer cunt and cheek;
Then, angry, they miscall me weak,
Till one, divining me aright,
Points to her buttocks, whispers "Greek!"—
A strong man's love is my delight!

Boys tempt my lips to wanton use,
And show their tongues, and smile awry,
And wonder why I should refuse
To feel their buttocks on the sly,
And kiss their genitals, and cry:
'Ah! Ganymede, grant me one night!'
This is the one sweet mystery:
A strong man's love is my delight!

To feel him clamber on me, laid
Prone on the couch of lust and shame,
To feel him force me like a maid
And his great sword within me flame,

His breath as hot and quick as fame;
To kiss him and to clasp him tight;
This is my joy without a name,
A strong man's love is my delight.

To feel again his love grow grand
Touched by the languor of my kiss;
To suck the hot blood from my gland
Mingled with fierce spunk that doth hiss,
And boils in sudden spurted bliss;
Ah! God! The long-drawn lusty fight!
Grant me eternity of this!
A strong man's love is my delight!

Envoi

Husband, come early to my bed,
And stay beyond the dawn of light
In mighty deeds of lustihead.
A strong man's love is my delight!

To A.D.

Across the sea that lies between us twain
I gaze and see thee, exiled but as free
As winds that lash the billows of the main
Across the sea.

I remain here in somber slavery
Amid these winter gusts of bitter pain,
And sorrow for thy lips in vain, in vain,
Bound by the world's inexorable chain,
And parted from thee. Spirit of Liberty,

Bear thou my kisses' sunshine, my tears' rain
To him I love, who may one day love me,
And bid him gladden at my amorous strain
Across the sea.

At Kiel

Oh, the white flame of limbs in dusky air,
The furnace of thy great grey eyes on me
Turned till I shudder. Darkness on the sea,
And wan ghost-lights are flickering everywhere
So that the world is ghastly. But within
Where we two cling together, and hot kisses
Stray to and fro amid the wildernesses
Of swart curled locks! I deem it a sweet sin,
So sweet that fires of hell have no more power
On body and soul to quench the lustrous flame
Of that desire that burns between us twain.
What is Eternity, seeing we hold this hour
For all the lusts and luxuries of shame?
Heaven is well lost for this surpassing gain.

Suggested Additional Stanzas for 'A Ballad of Burdens'

The burden of caught clap. How sore it is!
A burden of sad shameful suffering,
The bitter bastard of a bloody kiss,
The Parthian arrow poisoned from Love's sling!
Lo, sweet Lord Christ, thou knowest how sore a thing
Is a cock crooked and consumed of fire
Shooting out venomous sap that hath a sting!
This is the end of every man's desire.

The burden of bought boys. Behold, dear Lord,
How plump their buttocks be, lift up Thine eyes,
See how their cocks stand at an amorous word,
How their lips suck out life until love dies,
See, Lord, Thou knowest, how wearily one lies
Cursing the lusts that fail, the deeds that tire;
Shrunk is San Cresce to a sorry size.
This is the end of every man's desire.

'Go into the Highways and Hedges, and Compel Them to Come in'

Let my fond lips but drink thy golden wine,
My bright-eyed Arab, only let me eat
The rich brown globes of sacramental meat
Steaming and firm, hot from their home divine,
And let me linger with thy hands in mine,
And lick the sweat from dainty dirty feet
Fresh with the loose aroma of the street,
And then anon I'll glue my mouth to thine.

This is the height of joy, to lie and feel
Thy spicéd spittle trickle down my throat;
This is more pleasant than at dawn to steal
Toward lawns and sunny brooklets, and to gloat
Over earth's peace, and hear in ether float
Songs of soft spirits into rapture peal.

The Blood-Lotus[18]

The ashen sky, too sick for sleep, makes my face grey;
my senses swoon;
Here, in the glamour of the moon, will not some pitying
godhead weep
For cold grey anguish of her eyes, that look to God, and
look in vain,
For death, the anodyne of pain, for sleep, earth's trivial
paradise?

Sleep I forget. Her silky breath no longer fans my ears;
I dream I float on some forgotten stream that hath a sa-
vor still of death,
A sweet warm smell of hidden flowers whose heavy pet-
als kiss the sun,
Fierce tropic poisons every one that fume and sweat
through forest hours;
They grow in darkness, heat beguiles their sluggish
kisses, in the wood
They breathe no murmur that is good, and Satan in
their blossom smiles.

They murder with the old perfume that maddens all
men's blood; we die

---

18 The lotus flower has been used in sacred rites and observations dating
back to Ancient Egypt. It functions as a symbol in Buddhism and Islam. *Ne-
lumbo nucifera* or the aquatic lotus is used as ornamentation in ceremonies such
as the Songkran Festival in Thailand when thousands of white blooms enclasing
tea candles are scattered on lakes and coastal waters at night.

Fresh from some corpse-clothed memory, some secret redolence of gloom,

Some darkling murmurous song of lust quite strange to man and beast and bird,

Silent in power, not overheard by any snake that eats the dust:

No crimson-hooded viper knows, no silver-crested asp has guessed

The strange soft secrets of my breast; no leprous cobra shall disclose.

The many-seated, multiform, divine, essential joys that these

Dank odours bring, that starry seas wash white in vain; intense and warm

The scents fulfil, they permeate all lips, all arteries, and fire

New murmured music on the lyre that throbs the horrors they create.

Omniscient blossom! Is thy red slack bosom fresher for my kiss?

Are thy loves sharper? Hast thou bliss in all the sorrows of the dead?

Why art thou paler when the moon grows loftier in the troublous sky?

Why dost thou beat and heave when I press lips of fire, hell's princeliest boon,

To thy mad petals, green and gold like angels' wings, when as a flood

God's essence fills them, and the blood throughout their web grows icy cold?

To thy red centre are my eyes held fast and fervent, as at night
Some sad miasma lends a light of strange and silent blasphemies
To lure a soul to hell, to draw some saint's charred lust, to tempt, to win
Another sacrifice to sin, another poet's heart to gnaw
With dubious remorse. Oh! Flame of torturing flower-love! Sacrament
Of Satan, triple element of mystery and love and shame,
Green, gold, and crimson, in my heart you strive with Jesus for its realm,
While Sorrow's tears would overwhelm the warriors of either part!

Jesus would lure me: from his side the gleaming torrent of the spear
Withdraws, my soul with joy and fear waits for sweet blood to pour its tide
Of warm delight—in vain! So cold, so watery, so slack it flows,
It leaves me moveless as a rose, albeit her flakes are manifold.
He hath no scent to drive men mad; no mystic fragrance from his skin
Sheds a loose hint of subtle sin such as the queen Faustina had.

Thou drawest me. Thy golden lips are carven Cleopatra-wise
Large, full, and moist, within them lies the silver rampart, whence there slips

That rosy flame of love, the fount of blood at my light
bidding spilt;
And my desires, if aught thou wilt, are with thy mind,
and thy account
With God shall bear my name the more; give me the
knowledge, me the power
For some new sin one little hour, and bankrupt God the
creditor:

Steal from his stock of suffering; his tender mercies rob
at will;
Destroy his graciousness, until he must avenge the
name of king.
Strange fascinations whirl and wind about my spirit ly-
ing coils;
Thy charm enticeth, for the spoils of victory, all an evil
mind.
Thy perfume doth confound my thought, new longings
echo, and I crave
Doubtful liaisons with the grave and loves of Parthia for
sport,
I think perhaps no longer yet, but dream and lust for
stranger things
Than ever sucked the lips of kings, or fed the tears of
Mahomet.
Quaint carven vampire bats, unseen in curious hollows
of the trees,
Or deadlier serpents coiled at eased round carcasses of
birds unclean.

All wandering changeful spectre shapes that dance in
slow sweet measure round

And merge themselves in the profound, nude women
and distorted apes
Grotesque and hairy, in their rage more rampant than
the stallion steed;
There is no help; their horrid need on these pale women
they assuage.

Wan breasts too pendulous, thin hands waving so aim-
lessly, they breathe
Faint sickly kisses, and inweave my head in quiet burial-
bands.
The silent troops recede; within the fiery circle of their
glance
Warm writhing woman-horses dance a shameless Bac-
chanal of sin;
Foam whips their reeking lips, and still the flower-witch
nestles to my lips,
Twines her swart lissome legs and hips, half serpent and
half devil, till
My whole life seems to lie in her; her kisses draw my
breath; my face
Loses its lustre in the grace of her quick bosom; sinister

The raving spectres reel; I see beyond my Circe's eyes no
shape
Save vague cloud-measures that escape the dances
whirling witchery.
Their song is in my ears, that burn with their melodious
wickedness;
But in her heart my sorceress has songs more sinful,
that I learn

As she sings slowly all their shame, and makes me tingle with delight
At new debaucheries, whose might rekindles blood and bone to flame.
The circle gathers. Negresses howl in the naked dance, and wheel
On poniard-blades of poisoned steel, and weep out blood in agonies;
Strange beast and reptile writhe; the song grows high and melancholy now;

The perfume savours every brow with lust unutterable of wrong;
Clothed with my flower-bride I sit, a harlot in a harlot's dress,
And laugh with careless wickedness that strews the broad road of the Pit
With vine and myrtle and thy flower, my harlot-maiden, who for man
Now first forsakest thy leman, thy Eve, my Lilith, in this bower

Which we indwell, a deathless three, changeless and changing, as the pyre
Of earthly love becomes a fire to heat us through eternity.
I have forgotten Christ at last; he may look back, grown amorous,
And call across the gulf to us, and signal kisses through the vast;
We shall disdain, clasp vaster yet, and mock his newer pangs, and call

With stars and voices musical, jeers his touched heart shall not forget.

I would have pitied him. This flower spits blood upon him, so must I

Cast ashes through the misty sky to mock his faded crown of power,

And with our laughter's nails refix his torn flesh faster to the wood,

And with more cruel zest make good the shackles of the Crucifix.

So be it, in thy arms I rest, lulled into silence by the strain

Of sweet love-whispers, while I drain damnation from thy tawny breast.

Nor heed the haggards sun's eclipse, feeling thy perfume fill my hair,

And all thy dark caresses wear sin's raiment on thy melting lips—

Nay, by the witchcraft of thy charms to sleep, nor drain that

God survive;

To wake, this only to contrive—fresh passions in thy naked arms;

And, at that moment when thy breath mixes with mine, like wine, to call

Each memory, one merged into all, to kiss, to sleep, to mate with death!

To My First-Born

At last a father! In Mathilde's womb
The poison quickens, and the tare-seeds shoot;
On my old Upas tree a bastard fruit
Is grafted. One more generation's doom
Fixes its fangs. Crime's flame, disease's gloom,
Are thy birth-dower. Another prostitute
Predestined, born man, damned to grow a brute!
Another travels tainted to the tomb!

My sin, my madness, in thy blood are set,
A vile imperishable coronet,
To hound thee into hell! God spits at thee
The curse thy parents earned. Revenge be thine!
Kiss Lust, kill Truth, and worship at Sin's shrine.
And foul His face with dung—thy infamy!

Chant au Saint-Esprit

Bah! Gros bougre du ciel!
Tu ne te plais pas seulement
Des chansons de Gabriel,

Ni non plus du sacrament
Très banal, ni des anthemes;
Mais l'horrible hurlement

De mes curieux blasphèmes
Te plaira, je parierai!
Jesus dit ces anathemes:

'Vous ces choses qui direz,
'Blasphémant le Saint-Esprit,
'N'aurez pardon pour jamais!'

Néanmoins, Jésus, je dis!
Saint-Esprit, je crois à toi,
Suceur du callibistris

Du bon Dieu, ta douce loi
Moi je garderai toujours!
Salut, bon et puissant roi!

Je veux goûter tes amours,
Avoir ta belle Marie,
En la jouant les trois tours;

Derrière, et ventre aussi,
Et la belle bouche, après,
Quand je serai ramolli,

Ni la semer de bon blé,
Mais la sucer, si l'on ose
Apres toi; je n'aimerais

Comme toi, en plein nevrose,
Si je devine tes goûts,
La faire feuille-de-rose!

Eh, gros bougre? Es-tu fou
Que ta grosse bouche baise
(Quand la lune est moins aigue)

Le bon vin au goût des fraises
De ces nymphes si sanglantes—
Ce qu'on nomme 'les Anglaises'

Envie-tu ces amantes
Qui le culte de Sapho
Jouissent, petites tantes?

N'exiges-tu quelque impôt
Sur ces fours des Lesbiennes
Pour ton bon petit jambot?

Permets-tu que ces chiennes
Boivent de ta Marie miel,
Sans que leur p'tits culs tiennent

Memoire de tes autels?
Ai-je dit assez, bretteur,
Pour m'assurer de l'enfer?
Bah! gros bougre du ciel!

Victory

Ah, God! That thou has made me thus,
Content of nought, intent to attain
The summits of hills amorous,
The crests desired of all of us,

By that fierce superflux of pain,
That battling with strange enemies,
The awful holocaust of gain,
And golden rushing of men slain

Before Thy throne, whose woven lies,
Fixed by enchantment in the dome
Of fiery ether, burn with eyes
Insatiate of Paradise—

Fixed, if the curse of brackish foam
Upon the salt unpiteous sea
Be fixed, or if the faith of Rome
Shall find in hearts of men a home

While men are living, fair and free—
Ah me, since justice must endure
And draw her sword at last, and be
The eternal conqueror of Thee.

And I, shall my support be sure
In that great day of righteous war?
Is my soul free? Is my heart pure?
Shall life diseased in death find cure?

Or shall the shameless barren whore
That rules my ways be found my guide,
Wed in bad bands so foul and sore
That Liberty shall be not more

Within my heart or at my side?
O Pleasure, whom I made my god,
And based my forehead for thy pride
And took thy bastard for my bride,

Subdued my shoulders to thy rod,
Casting before thy feet the things,
The virtues that thou didst hate; I trod
A bloody winepress, and went shod

With glorious feet stained through with rings,
Kissed blood that leapt to feel the tongue
Slip eager through the teeth, while clings
The lissome body, borne on wings

Of pain unspeakable, unsung,
To that tormentor, red and cruel,
Those teeth that bit for joy, and clung
Murderously amorous, while the young

Tender flesh burned, a quivering fuel
For strange desire, for strange desire,
Passion and penitence, and dule,
Love glowing some unholy jewel

Glittering frightful mid the mire.
Oh! Love, what utter sweetness yet!
What agony of curst hell-fire,
Shame, lust, and infamy, and ire,

Wrath in the highest heavens set,
Shame in the soul, and leaping lust
On pleasure's flaming parapet,
An Infamy that I forget.

As swords that flash forget the rust
That clings them round, as fighting men
Forget their wounds, with no distrust
Of death. Yea, dust may turn to dust,

Man's spirit to his God again,
But memory cannot fade, and while
My hot devouring kisses rain
On thy worn face, in writhing pain

Biting my lips, that fiercely smile
As tigers' lips, and gnaw thy mouth,
Till the blood spurts in dainty style
And blinds and bruises me awhile,

Yet satiates the awful drouth;
I suck, and shudder, and rave, and clutch,
Thy breasts, with wounds and sores uncouth,
Drenched with diseases of the south,

The hot south lands, where crooked crutch,
The leprous arm, the withered hand,
Bear sway, where thou wast nurtured, such
A queen as men delight to touch.

And I, between the wastes of sand
In one great harbour by a well,
Met thee, princess of such a band
Of merchantmen; my curved brand

Then was raised high, as wild of yell,
We flashed and charged, and slew thy folk;
Thou camest to my bed to dwell—
That day there clanged the gates of hell

Behind us twain; we never spoke
Save of love's bidding we might do,
Save on our lust to place a yoke
Too bitter to be lightly broke.

Each might we drew on, and something new
Of lust we learnt, insatiate we
Who wrote in blood the volumes through
That speak of love. But then there grew

A giant lust, strong as the sea;
And we with fresh delight assayed
The fierce sweet bond of tribady,
The strange strong sin of sodomy,

And thus from foe to foe betrayed,
No pain or pleasure but we knew
Its utterest essence, whence we made
All agonies, that God has paid

With rotting blood, save one, that few
Could dream of, so divine it is,
So exquisite, so rich to do,
The which tonight we meet unto—

To consummate the angry bliss
Of all excesses of delight;
The pain of this divine disease,
The luxury of the obscene kiss,

The carnal anguish, and the sight
Of sore bloody breasts and thighs,
The bright green river foamed with white,
The horrid spasms of the night.

Long have we lusted on this wise;
Now one delight, the last is left—
Come, I will lick thine haggard eyes,
And wallow on thee straddle-wise.

Here with thy fingers fierce and deft,
Take me, all bloody as it is,
And plunge within thy furious cleft
My fierce red pillar to the heft!

Suck deep the poison. Now I wish
The sweet pollution of thy breath
Was never so divine! Thy Kiss!
Ah, sweet Lord Christ! So sweet as this!
Ah, Christ! Together! Passion! Death!

Sleeping in Carthage

The month of thirst is ended. From the lips
That hide their blushes in the golden wood
A fervent fountain amorously slips,
The dainty rivers of thy luscious blood;
Red streams of sweet nepenthe that eclipse
The milder nectar that the gods hold good—
How my dry throat, held hard between thy hips,
Shall drain the moon-wrought flow of womanhood!

Divinest token of sterility,
Strange barren fountain blushing from the womb,
Like to an echo of Augustan gloom
When all men drank this wine; it maddens me
With yearnings after new divinity,
Prize of thy draught, somewhere beyond the tomb.

With Dog and Dame, an October Idyll

The ways are golden with the leaves
That autumn blows about the air,
The trees sing anthems of despair,
And my fair mistress binds the sheaves
Of yellow hair more loose, and weaves
More subtly bars of song, that bear
Bright children of love debonair,
And laughter lightly comes, and reaves
The garland from our sorrow's brow,
Life rises up, is girt with song,
Joy fills the cup, that flashes clear.
The year may fade in whispers now,
Shadow and silence now may throng
The seasons—we are happy here.

Autumn is on us as we lie
In creamy clouds of latticed light
That hint at darkness, but descry
A rosy flicker through the night,
My mistress, my great Dane, and I.

We linger in the dusk—her head
Lolls on the pillow, and my eyes
Catch rapture, as upon the bed
He licks her lazy lips, and tries
To tempt her tongue. My fires are fed.

Her heavy dropping breasts entice
My teeth to jewel them with blood,
Her hand prepares the sacrifice
She would desire of me, the flood

That wells from shrines of Paradise.

Her other hand is mischievous
To bid the monster Dane grow mad,
His red-haw gaze grows mutinous,
Her eyes have lost the calm they had,
My body grows all amorous.

My tongue within her mouth excites
Her dirtiest lust, her vilest dream;
His greedy mouth her bosom bites;
He cannot hold, his eyeballs gleam;
He burns to consummate the rites.

I yield him place: his ravening teeth
Cling hard to her—he buries him
Insane and furious in the sheath
She opens for him—wide and dim
My mouth is amorous beneath.

Her lips devour me, and I rave
With pleasure to discern the love
They twain exert, my lips who lave
With doubled dew distilled above;
To dog and woman I'm a slave,

Nor move, though now essays the Dane
To cool his weapon in my mouth;
Her lust bestrides me, and is fain
To quench in his sweet sweat her drought
Her finger probes my bowel again.

All three enjoy once more, and I
Am ready ever to renew
These bestial orgy-nights, whereby

Loose woman's love is spiced, as dew
On tender spray of spring doth lie.

Like the cold moon to earth and sun
My mistress lingers in eclipse,
We wake her passion, either one
Licking each pouting pair of lips
Till new sweet streams of nectar run.

'Tis autumn, and the dying breeze
Murmurs 'embrace;' the moon replies
'Embrace;' the soughing of the trees
Calls us to linger loverwise,
And drain our passion to the lees.

'Tis autumn. The belated dove
Calls through the beeches, that bestir
Themselves to kiss the skies above,
As I will kiss with him and her.
Leave us, sweet Autumn, to our love.

Hermaphrodite's Dream

Ἐρμαφροδίτου ’Ὀ ναρ

I know that winged sprite
Who flew from heaven—was it hell?—
Into these bounds of light
And music—yesternight—
Had some new song to tell.

I saw a living soul
Flame into mortal dress;
Whose glance—a fiery coal,
Whose lips—a ruby bowl
Whose wine was wickedness.

They were strange lips, I ween,
Whereon no kiss might be,
And teeth were sharp therein;
Ivory and white and keen,
Tameless as hungering sea.

Strange body of my desire,
Voluptuous, lithe, and wan;
For, on my eyes drawn nigher,
My hot blood turns to fire,
Seeing nor maid nor man.

Not maid, not man—the breast
Like palaces of gold,
Yet where my lips caressed,
In the wild dove's wild nest

A dove too soft to hold.

No dove that Hylas knew,
No dove that Sappho kissed,
Nor in wide Heaven there grew
This child of stranger dew
Than God's good spirit wished.

Yet his wings bare him high,
Divine beyond control,
And, like for love to die,
I felt his arrow fly
Within my very soul.

Ah Love! the ambiguous kiss,
Not man's nor woman's touch,
In that ecstatic bliss—
Not hell's heat, as I wish,
Had warmed us overmuch.

Ah! Love! how fierce that night!
With what unsung desire
Thy lips and mouth were bright,
In mine eye to give light,
And fire to kindle fire.

Ah Love! Nor king nor queen
Of mine exhaustless flame,
But comrade of my teen,
Spouse of that epicene
Incontinence of shame.

Twin Love! Soul's dual spouse,
Dream-serpent of my life,
Rose-garland of my brows

Within that ivory house,
Sex with itself at strife.

Were I a wanton stream,
Thou mightest bathe in me,
Yet in that happy dream
Me thought my heart did deem
We mingled utterly.

O sexless! Deathless! Fair
Beyond the world to me,
Thy love-gift I will wear,
Thy joys my soul shall share,
Being made one with thee.

So, love, the days may keep
My nameless love from me;
Yet over slumber's deep
I will sail into sleep
Thither to lie by thee,

Hold thee with arms that cleave
Lock thee in limbs that leap,
Chain thee with lips that leave
Kisses of blood to weave
Castles of hope in sleep.

Poppy! Best flower whose bud
Sends dreams to men that die,
I drain thy drowsy flood
That our impatient blood
May mingle utterly.

So, Hermes, thou art wed,
So, Aphrodite, mine,

In one sweet spirit shed
In one ambrosial bed,
In one fair frame divine.

Like clouds in rain, like seas
Exultant as they roll,
We mix in ecstasies,
And, as breeze melts in breeze,
Thy soul becomes my soul.

I come to thee with tears,
Nameless immortal dove;
Forget the fleet-foot years
In the incarnate spheres
Of our mysterious Love.

'Erebus'

Something of monstrous in our love, our bed,
Soothes me with strong desire,
Strong but availing nothing—black and red
Thy body gleams, as fire
Thy great eyes burn, thy lips respire
It seems unnatural breath within their tomb.
Ah! the red portals of thy dusky womb,
Wherein my loves expire,
'Twixt thy black breasts to rise, kissed hard by thee
Till joy flows full once more, salt river to sweet sea.

Fairer than roses are thy swarthy cheeks,
Thine hair more sharp than gold;
Purple is warmer than mere red, when seeks
My love thy lips to hold.
Ah Queen! That other's breasts are cold
Being of wafted snowflakes beside thine;
Her breasts give milk as thine the fiercest wine;
Her ivory thighs enfold
Limbs not so amorous as these that lie
By the dark limbs, and lust for their imperial dye.

Thy mouth takes me within its eager lips;
My mouth thirsts, drinking long
Deep from the fount of love, whence out there slips
An eager purple tongue,
Sweet as the taste of summer song
From thrush's tender throat, a tongue that tires
My thirsty lips with its insatiate fires,

While swart limbs soft and strong
Grip my hot head, while thy lips kiss away
With blood and foam the life from him thou wouldst not
slay.

La Juive

Rose dotted with grey stars the bed
Where my fair Jewess lay and smiled:
Her breasts were full, her eyes were red,
Her lips with God unreconciled.
In wanton disarray, her hair
Streamed jetty black—Ah! God, how fair!

The quilt had gold embroidery,
About the room were furs and silk:
Her eyes were full of devilry,
Her finger-tips were soft as milk:
Above the bed a crest was set,
A gold and sapphire coronet.

She was of noble birth, and—best—
A Jewess; her bad lips enticed
My lips to taste; I held her breast
Fresh from the crucifying Christ;
It seemed her thighs were hot with blood
Sucked from the bastard Son of God.

I saw his broken body hang
Sweating and bleeding on the cross;
I heard his curses champ and clang;
I spat upon his reeking corpse;
I licked the spear; my feet were shod
With iron as I kicked my God.

Such frightful fancies dim my eyes—
I can remember how his side
Lay open for a lover's prize—

I violate the Crucified!
Hell shrieks with impious laugh; they sing
A mad lewd chant; Hell hails me king!

So runs my dream; but what am I?
A lover by a Jewess' bed,
A lover waiting wistfully
For his desires to be fed;
His only lust—a lover's bliss,
And with no language but a kiss!

In her loose lusts I find again
The memory of that dream gone by;
Her kisses waken in my brain
The picture of that infamy,
The low dark hill, the storm, the star
That lit my bestial lupanar!

Her breasts are Golgotha to me!
Her lips, his dripping hands and feet!
Her secret-cinctured armoury
Of pleasures seems—how utter sweet!—
The gaping spear-wound in his side
Wherein I smote the Crucified!

Come, night! dip, shadows! Only let
One incense-flame burn red and low,
Regild the golden coronet,
Gleam on her nude lewd hips, and glow
On hours of weariless desire,
A bastard and infernal fire.

Smite me, my fiend-fair whore, nor spare
My raging hips, but wake again
The old desires ere I'm aware,

Joy more intense from cruel pain:
They say he hoped his crown to fix
By his delirious crucifix.

Yes, spare me not, red-lipped, low browed,
Large-featured animal I love:
Prolong the orgie, shriek aloud
With drunken vehemence above
All violence more than Corybant
To our Iacchian God—Absinthe!

Ah! Thy red lips, and its green glint!
Its wavy splendour, and the dance
Thy belly weaves, a triple hint
Of Hell, and Algiers, and France!
Ah! Judas-love! This flask we'll drain,
Kiss hard—and so to bed again!

Necrophilia

Void of the ecstasies of Art
It were in life to have lain by thee,
And felt thy kisses rain on me,
And the hot beating of thy heart,

When thy warm sweat should leave me cold,
And my worn soul find out no bliss
In the obscenities I kiss,
And the things shameful that I hold.

My nostrils sniff the luxury
Of flesh decaying, bowels torn
Of festive worms, like Venus, born
Of entrails foaming like the sea.

Yea, thou art dead. Thy buttocks now
Are swan-soft, and thou sweatest not;
And hast a strange desire begot
In me, to lick thy bloody brow;

To gnaw thy hollow cheeks, and pull
Thy lustful tongue from out its sheath;
To wallow in the bowels of death,
And rip thy belly, and fill full

My hands with all putridities;
To chew thy dainty testicles;
To revel with the worms in Hell's
Delight in such obscenities;

To pour within thine heart the seed
Mingled with poisonous discharge
From a swollen gland, inflamed and large
With gonorrhea's delicious breed;

To probe thy belly, and to drink
The godless fluids, and the pool
Of rank putrescence from the stool
Thy hanged corpse gave, whose luscious stink

Excites these songs sublime. The rod
Gains new desire; dive, howl, cling, suck,
Rave, shriek, and chew; excite the fuck,
Hold me, I come! I'm dead! My God!

Abysmos

Αβνσμος

This is th' abyss! Implacable disease
Springs from the black defilement of that kiss,
That foul embrace that moulds these agonies.
This is th' abyss!

A serpent was my whore; her hellish hiss,
Her slaver venoms soul and strength; life flees
Repugnant from the corpse-caress. Ah, this

Rots blood and body; see, the liquor's lees
I drained, whose pangs are fierce with Syphilis.
Christ God, damn soul, but quench the pain of these!
This is th' abyss!

* * *

This is th' abyss. Behold wherein I lurk
The lazar-house my mind, wherein do work
The horrid charnel-priests, whose loathly song
Sickens my soul, and quells the spirit strong.
Hell-fire within my heart! And poisoned blood
Through every vein and artery pours a flood
Of devilish pain. This is th' abyss indeed;
Fears on my mind and pains on body feed,

Serpents of hell that gnaw my bones, nor quench
The fires of torture with the sickly stench

Of many a venomed drug, that clings and cleaves,
An clutches like a dead man's hand, and weaves
Its subtle scheme of agony through me.
Is God to help a mortal? Or are we
Caught in Fate's mesh without a hope to 'scape?

Ah! Look around! In every darksome shape!
Fearful, nude Venus grins. Alcyone
Mocks with her sickening smile. Hill, moor, and lea
Make me to hate them. Only Clytie there,
Wild arms thrown wide, an agony of hair
Streamed fierce behind her, seems to sympathize;
Through selfish, yet despair in both our eyes
Gives us a link of love. The darkling room
Is fearsome; one red light throughout the gloom
Thrills my void veins with horror. On the couch
The gruesome hound with sleepy stare doth crouch.

His red hard eye upon me. Every shelf
Of noisome books reflects my hideous self!
Lucky I burnt my picture! Snakes on floor
Writhe, lick my legs, I fear them. By the door
Yon horrid panther snarls. His eye inspires
Fresh torments, to invade my soul with fires
Too angry to assuage, and in its glass
I see myself. I hate myself, alas!

More than all these. I cannot rid me of
Myself, my hates, my tortures, or my love;
My golden-haired Greek goddess, who divines
In me a god, who cannot read the lines
Of anguish on my forehead, neither scent

The poison of breast, blood, and excrement!
I gnash my teeth in impotent despair
That I may never hold her heavenly hair
Again, nor bite her lips, as once my teeth
Met in her cheek, to cull a rosy wreath
Of blood upon it, nor assuage the pangs
Of love with hardy limbs, and dolorous fangs,
And sweating body, crimsoning with gore,
As her mad mouth devoured me. Never more
Though years decay! With them my blood decays,
My bones rot inwardly, the venomed days

Sink shaft on shaft of agony, the years
Bring new distortions, miseries, and fears;
New torture to my spirit, and forgot
Of God, and health, and loveliness, I rot.
Outward, my face and breast have leprous sores;
Inward, my filthy blood; its poison pours
Corruption through me. In the eyes of man
I am contemned, the haughty one. God's fan
Is eager on my threshing-floor; his rod
Smites no vain stroke. Oh, how I curse thee, God!

What is my aid? But yet to Satan's power
I lend my utmost vigour for an hour,
To wrest Thy damned throne from out thy hands!
My aid? How shall I burst thy bitter bands,
Strike off thy shackles, from thy fetters break,
I, whom Thy name appals, whose vitals quake
At the dim thought of Thee? Have mercy, Christ!
Who suffered on the cross, who sacrificed
Thy heaven for three hours. Ah! pity me,
For years, not hours, condemned to agony

Thrice Thine ! Have pity, hear me, virgin queen,
Whose pangs of childbirth were seven times
more keen
Than all, since love and memory of joy
Thou hadst not, but the fear of shame to cloy
Even the hope of motherhood. But I,
Cut off from love and joy; its memory
One black hell of distorted pain; my shame
More horrid than that first unholy flame,
That burnt my blood, and flung me in her arms,
Whose filthy kisses and thrice loathly charms,
Her purple lips, her acrid redolence,
Her black lewd limbs, her breasts, whose foul incense
Smoked like hell's mouth though pendulous
they hung,
Her devilish black belly, and her tongue
Sharp as a tiger's tooth, lured on my lust.
Oh! God in heaven! It is turned to dust

And dung and corpse-flesh! I can see even here
(For changeful spectres haunt me) how a tear
Of blood stood on my breast at her first bite:
And day grew dusk, and twilight turned to night,
And her vast coffin stood at hand. And there
Naked as hell, legs wide flung out in the air,
She lay and called me 'Satan'. As I came,
Feeling a Satan, such a deathly flame
Of lust of loathliness was kindled here
In my bad blood, I leapt upon the bier,
And consummated all the strange desire
That burnt and branded all my blood with fire,
Buried my teeth and limbs in swarthy flesh,
While blood and sweat begat desire afresh,
And yet twelve times the black womb vomited,

And we lay there chilled bitterly, and dead,
While thy lewd minions covered with a pall
Our prostrate bodies, and with musical
Loud voices raised the chant of funeral,
Turned to fierce blasphemies, and words obscene.
Nine hours we lay as dead, and then my queen
Writhed in my arms again, and blood leapt up
To our fresh kisses to fill full the cup
Of horror to the brim. Again as dead
Were we borne forth, and then—Can I forget?
I gripped thy glossy throat. My fingers met

Crushing through the skin and muscle,
nerve and vein,
And in that supreme agony of pain
I drained myself of lust! That final clasp
Was consummated in thy dying gasp!
The frightful struggle ended; I leapt high,
Caught sword, bared breast,
and hurled myself to die,
But thy mad slaves attacked me. These I slew
—So I half guess—the next thing my soul knew,
I was alone and naked in my bed.
The sword, snapped, on the floor, with hateful red
Blotches of blood, and clots of bloody hair
On its infernal steel. And unaware
Of thy last gift I slept. I have it now,
Thy gift from Hell's door! Would to God somehow
I had thee once alive—to slay again!—
Ah! Who crawls in upon me like a vain
Damned ghost? Ugh! Blotchy spectre! Fiend, aroint!
Ah Christ, he creeps toward me; every joint
Quivers with passion; he will tear my eyes!
Away! More liquor! Come, green cockatrice!

Come, filthy draught of fire! Green dancing fiend
On serpent's vomit and whore's spittle weaned,
Fire my fierce brain! Resolve my rotted heart!
Fill me with drunkenness! How changed thou art,
Body, from that these women loved so well!
God! Will they still lust after me in Hell?

But this is Hell! Aha! If you were me,
Blind staring cripple yonder, you should see
Whether I lie! A cripple are you then?
Look upon me, the leper among men,
The corpse among the living! Intercede,
Good pitying pitiable Christ! My need
Is viler than my sins! Old sins, you tire!
Come, some new devilry to reinspire
My lips with frenzied laughter! Vain, ah, vain!
Th' extreme of pleasure and the worst of pain,
I have tasted all. No more, all hope must end—
Hope! Damn that word! It mocks me like that friend
Who comes to see me daily—I shall die
Happier if I kill him; so shall I
Reap on his body the last tare of lust,
And shrivel back into my primal dust
Filled with all worms and hornéd beasts with wings,
The reptile that sweats acrid juice, and stings
With bloody teeth and tongue! Oh, all the room
Spits fire and dung, and vomits forth a spume
Of tawny sickly death! All blotched and dark,
The putrid air is vital with a spark
Of fiery eyes of yonder filthy hound!
God! I am reeling brain and body! I swound!
The floor heaves up! The worms devour my breast!
Beasts and lewd fish and wingèd things infest

Each vital part! Screech, rats! More liquor! Come!
Rumble, you rotting whore-skin of a drum!
I care not! Scream, you rats! Snakes, bite and hiss!
Hell's spawn, I mouth you with this putrid kiss!
Satan! Damnation! This is the abyss!

Made in the USA
Middletown, DE
01 December 2021